discovermore

Life in a Community

Types of Communities

Dwayne Hicks

Britannica Educational Publishing

IN ASSOCIATION WITH

THE ROSEN PUBLISHING GROUP

Published in 2024 by Britannica Educational Publishing (a trademark of Encyclopædia Britannica, Inc.) in association with The Rosen Publishing Group, Inc.
2544 Clinton Street, Buffalo, NY 14224

Distributed exclusively by Rosen Publishing.
To see additional Britannica Educational Publishing titles, go to rosenpublishing.com.

Editor: Kathleen Klatte
Book Design: Leslie Taylor

Photo Credits: Cover Rawpixel.com/Shutterstock.com; (series background) Dai Yim/Shutterstock.com; p. 5 (top) SARIN KUNTHONG/Shutterstock.com, (bottom) haveseen/Shutterstock.com; p. 6 ESB Professional/Shutterstock.com; p. 7 Mike Liu/Shutterstock.com; p. 8 Atstock Productions/Shutterstock.com; p. 9 Belish/Shutterstock.com; p. 11 (top) Jose F. Donneys/Shutterstock.com, (bottom) Dominick Corrado/Shutterstock.com; p. 12 Smit/Shutterstock.com; p. 13 Patrick Jennings/Shutterstock.com; p. 14 Jose Luis Stephens/Shutterstock.com; p. 15 SpeedKingz/Shutterstock.com; p. 16 Rebekah Zemansky/Shutterstock.com; p. 17 Joseph Sohm/Shutterstock.com; p. 18 The Brownfowl collection/Shutterstock.com; p. 19 T photography/Shutterstock.com; p. 21 (top) Jai Mayers/Shutterstock.com, (bottom) pisaphotography/Shutterstock.com; p. 23 (top) Zunkir/https://commons.wikimedia.org/wiki/File:Complaint_tablet_to_Ea-Nasir_2020.jpg, (bottom) Chris Colbert/Shutterstock.com; p. 24 S.Borisov/Shutterstock.com; p. 25 Sean Pavone/Shutterstock.com; p. 26 Creative Supreme NYC/Shutterstock.com; p. 27 Pierre Jean Durieu/Shutterstock.com; p. 28 4kclips/Shutterstock.com; p. 29 Dmytro Zinkevych/Shutterstock.com.

Library of Congress Cataloging-in-Publication Data

Names: Hicks, Dwayne.
Title: Types of communities / Dwayne Hicks.
Description: New York : Britannica Educational Publishing, in Association with Rosen Educational Services. 2024. | Series: Discover more: life in a community | Includes glossary and index.
Identifiers: ISBN 9781642828870 (library bound) | ISBN 9781642828863 (pbk) | ISBN 9781642828887 (ebook)
Subjects: LCSH: Communities--Juvenile literature.
Classification: LCC HM756.H53 2024 | DDC 307–dc23

Manufactured in the United States of America

Contents

Different Kinds of Communities 4
Urban Communities.................... 6
Suburban Communities 10
Rural Communities 12
Your Community's Government 16
Moving Around the Community 20
Our Changing Communities 22
Communities Within Communities..... 26
Glossary 30
For More Information 31
Index 32

Different Kinds of Communities

A community is a group of people who live in the same area and share resources. Humans can be a part of many different kinds of communities. Each community affects how its members live their daily lives. For instance, if you live in a city, or urban community, you could see hundreds of people every day. But if you live in a rural community, you may see a dozen people every day.

A city is a concentrated center of population that includes a variety of workplaces, schools, and residential buildings. Built-up areas called suburbs lie outside the boundaries of most big cities. Rural communities are in the countryside. There are fewer homes there, spread farther apart.

In an urban community, you might live in an apartment, with lots of neighbors in the same building.

compareandcontrast

Which kind of community would you prefer to live in—urban, suburban, or rural? Why?

In a rural community, the nearest neighbors might be a mile or more down the road.

Urban Communities

In a city, many people live and work very close together. New York City is the largest city in the United States. Other big American cities are Los Angeles, Chicago, and Houston. Toronto is the biggest city in Canada. Tokyo, Japan, has more people than any other metropolitan area in the world.

A city's central business district, or downtown, usually has its tallest office buildings and biggest stores. The downtown area is often the oldest part of the city.

Tokyo has many tall buildings to accommodate its dense population.

People travel from all over the world to see concerts, operas, and ballets at Lincoln Center in New York City.

A city usually has one or more areas with factories and warehouses (storage buildings) outside of downtown. Most of the city's homes lie still farther from downtown.

Cities usually have a variety of places for entertainment and relaxation. People travel from all over the world to see famous theaters and **museums** in big cities like New York and London.

WORD WISE

A museum is a place where interesting or valuable objects, such as artwork, are collected for people to view.

Cities can be wonderful places to live, work, or visit. Cities bring together a great variety of people from different backgrounds. They attract people looking for work, education, and other ways to improve their lives. They bring together many talented people. Cities are therefore often centers of invention, artistic creation, acceptance, and social change.

City life can also be hard. Not everyone shares equally in the benefits of the city. Some people live in rundown, overcrowded housing. Others have no homes at all. They sometimes live on the streets.

In a big city, you might see people shopping, eating in restaurants, or going to the theater.

You might also see homeless people.

Crowded living conditions in cities sometimes also lead to crime, heavy traffic, and pollution.

Many people in cities work to try to solve these problems. Local governments and private groups provide funds to operate homeless shelters and soup kitchens. Community organizations try to make life better for people who live in the less fortunate areas of cities.

Consider This

List five things that are easier to do in a city than in a suburb or rural community.

Suburban Communities

The area surrounding a major city is called its metropolitan area. Suburban communities are part of that area. Suburbs may be towns, villages, or small cities. They have their own local governments and services such as police and fire protection. People who live in the suburbs often commute, or travel for work, to the city. This is because cities supply many of the jobs for people who live in the suburbs.

There are many differences between life in a city and life in a suburb. People often move from the city to the suburbs as they get older and have children because they want more space. The suburbs usually offer larger homes with grassy yards and better-funded public schools. Suburban residents often need cars to move around their own communities.

Westchester County is a suburb of New York City. People who live there can commute to the city by train. They might also drive to work in New Jersey.

compare**and**contrast

Would you rather live in a major metropolitan city or a smaller, suburban city? Why?

Some suburban towns can be very expensive places to live.

Rural Communities

You might hear people refer to rural communities as being "out in the country." They are large areas of land with few houses or businesses. They often do not have as many services as cities and suburbs. People may have to travel long distances to the nearest grocery store, doctor, or school.

Rural areas can be great places to see the stars and other celestial objects. There are no bright city lights to cause a distraction.

Farms that raise crops or livestock take up a lot of space. That's why the nearest neighbors might be a few miles away.

There are many reasons people like living in rural communities. Some enjoy the peace and quiet. Others appreciate being close to nature and outdoor activities, such as hunting, fishing, and hiking. Many rural residents appreciate the slower pace of life and the cheaper cost of living. While rural communities are small, they are usually close-knit. People depend on and help out their neighbors. Some rural households aren't connected to services like a community water system. They might get their water from a well and use a septic system for sewage.

Consider This

Most rural American areas have access to high-speed internet. Think of all the things you do with the internet. What else do you think a rural farmer might use it for?

People in rural areas often work outdoors. Farmers grow food and raise animals. Some people work in logging, cutting down trees. The wood from the trees is used to make lumber for building things or turned into pulp that is used to make paper. Other people extract fossil fuels, such as oil, coal, and natural gas. Some rural areas are major sources of mineral resources, such as copper and iron ore.

Mining is a dangerous occupation. Mines create a lot of pollution.

Responsible forestry means planting new trees to replace the ones that are cut down for lumber.

These job options mean that rural life can be hard. Advances in **agriculture** have reduced the need for human workers on farms and ranches. The coal mining and logging industries are struggling, too. People have moved away from some rural areas because of that. Some people keep vacation homes in rural areas. They work in the city most of the time. Or they might work remotely from a rural home, via the internet.

WORD WISE

Agriculture is the science and business of farming.

Your Community's Government

Local communities are run by municipal governments. A municipality is a city, town, or village that is self-governing. In some cases, a county can be a municipality. Counties are called boroughs in Alaska and parishes in Louisiana.

The structure of municipal governments varies from country to country. In the United States, it also varies from state to state. A municipal government for a town may include a group of elected lawmakers called a town council.

Residents make their opinions known at a city council meeting.

The town hall is usually located downtown, in a central part of the community. It might be near other public buildings, such as the library or police station.

One for a city would be called a city council. Many municipalities elect a leader called a mayor. In some towns the mayor has a lot of power, while in others the mayor is just the chairperson of the town council. Some cities also have a city manager. This is a hired executive who's trained in the business of running a city.

Consider This

Who's in charge of your local government? A mayor? Town council? County executive?

Your local government provides many services to the community. These include police and fire protection, hospitals, and schools. Many municipalities collect residents' garbage, clear snow from roads, and build and maintain streets, sidewalks, parks, and playgrounds.

Different municipalities provide different services. The larger the municipality, the more services it is called upon to provide. Large cities have their own libraries, museums, zoos, historical societies, and other cultural attractions. To attract and keep businesses, they often build sports arenas and convention centers.

A large community might have a police headquarters and perhaps its own police academy. A small town might have a single police station.

New York City has an elaborate park system that includes zoos, skating rinks, and playgrounds.

Municipalities pay for services by charging fees and collecting taxes from the people who live there. Wealthy communities are able to provide more services than poorer ones. A wealthy community might hire landscapers to plant pretty shrubs and flowers on public land. A small or poor community might make do with sweeping the streets.

Consider This

Why do you think it might be more important to have a botanical garden in a major city than in a rural community?

Moving Around the Community

People need to move around the community for school, work, and many other reasons. They depend on various forms of transportation to get where they need to go. On top of these almost-daily trips, people also need to get to stores to buy food, clothes, and other goods. When they are sick or hurt, people need to get to a hospital or doctor.

Cities commonly have a public transportation system to help people get around without cars. Public transportation includes buses, trains, subways, and streetcars. Subways are trains that run underground. Streetcars run along tracks in a street. In rural areas and suburbs, most people depend on their own cars and trucks to get around. Many municipalities provide school buses to transport kids to and from school.

Street cars, or trolleys, are sort of like buses that run on tracks in the street.

compareandcontrast

Which do you think is better for the environment: taking a long trip in your car, or traveling by bus or train?

Many train lines connect at Grand Central Station in New York City. People can travel within the city, out to the suburbs, or even to other states.

Our Changing Communities

Like everything else, communities change over time. The first settlers in different areas around the world had to find safe places to live, with available resources, such as water, building materials, and good land for farming. Over time, roads and footpaths developed between villages as people traded with one another. Some villages grew into towns or cities.

About 5,500 years ago people in Mesopotamia (now Iraq) started the first cities. Some cities in ancient times were independent of any country. These city-states ruled themselves. Athens and Sparta were major city-states of ancient Greece. From the 1000s to the 1400s, Florence, Venice, and other city-states were important in today's Italy. Later, city-states lost their independence. Today most people consider Singapore, Monaco, and the Vatican to be the last remaining city-states.

One of the oldest pieces of written communication is from Mesopotamia. It's a complaint about a copper merchant from 1750 BCE.

compareandcontrast

How were ancient cities like modern ones? How were they different?

The Vatican is an independent city-state within the city of Rome, Italy.

One of the biggest factors in the growth of modern cities was the Industrial Revolution. New machines invented during this period made **manufacturing** an important business. Many people from the countryside moved into cities. They looked for work in newly built factories.

In the late 1800s, architects invented new building methods that changed the way cities looked. Tall buildings called skyscrapers appeared in many cities. During the 1900s, cities continued to change. They grew rapidly in population. They also spread outward. Many people moved to the suburbs. Some highly populated areas became known as megalopolises. Megalopolises often include several cities and many suburbs.

The city of Rome is thousands of years old. Today, you can see ancient ruins next to cars on modern streets.

In this picture of Boston, Massachusetts, you can see how the city has changed over the centuries.

Today, urban and suburban areas are growing more quickly than rural ones. This is likely because more jobs are available in urban and suburban communities. Industries that deal directly with the public, such as food service, health care, and retail sales provide many jobs in cities.

WORD WISE

Manufacturing is the business of making products, particularly in factories.

Communities Within Communities

Did you know that you can belong to more than one community at a time? After all, any group of people with a common interest or shared experience is a community. The people who are students or teachers at a particular school make up a school community. They all want to make their school a safe, welcoming place to learn.

Many Jewish people live in Brooklyn, New York. Some of them wear special clothing to show which community they belong to.

Native American communities preserve their lifestyle and customs.

People from the same background make up a community too. For example, a person might be a member of the African American community, the Italian-American community, or the Puerto Rican community.

Religion also creates communities. Examples include the Jewish, Muslim, and Hindu communities. The people who go to a particular house of worship make up a religious community, too. Nuns, monks, or priests who live somewhat apart from society form a different type of religious community.

Consider This

What kind of communities do you belong to? Are any of them ethnic or religious? Do they preserve any special traditions?

Throughout history, people have always formed communities. Members of the army, navy, and air force are part of the military community. Musicians are members of the general music community. They also belong to a community of a specific genre (or type) of music such as the hip-hop community or the country music community. People don't even need to meet in person to be part of a community. People who talk to each other online make up online communities.

A sorority is a community that exists within the larger community of a college campus.

These people are picking up trash in their community. This makes it a nicer place for everyone who lives there.

There are lots of things you can do to improve your communities. Make an effort to be friendly to a new neighbor, classmate, or teammate. Consider volunteering to pick up trash or visit a **nursing home**. Donate food or clothes to those in need. No matter what types of communities you belong to, the people who make up the community are what makes it special.

WORD WISE

A nursing home is a place where sick or elderly people live with staff to take care of them. People who enjoy crafts or playing bingo might form communities within the population of the nursing home.

Glossary

arena: An enclosed area used for public entertainment.

botanical garden: A large usually public garden where plants are grown in order to be studied.

communication: The act or process of using words, sounds, signs, or behaviors to express or exchange information or to express your ideas, thoughts, feelings, etc., to someone else.

concentrated: Existing or happening together in one place; not spread out.

convention center: A big building designed to hold large meetings.

factory: A building or group of buildings where products are made.

fossil fuel: A fuel (like coal, oil, or natural gas) that is formed in the earth from plant or animal remains.

homeless shelter: A place where people who have no home can stay.

municipality: A self-governing city or town.

population: The total number of people living in a country or region.

ranch: A place for raising livestock like cattle, horses, or sheep.

soup kitchen: A place that gives free food to the needy.

tax: Money the government collects to pay for services.

transportation: Methods for moving people and their goods from one place to another.

volunteer: A person who does work without getting paid to do it.

For More Information

Books

Ruurs, Margriet. *Where We Live: Mapping Neighborhoods of Kids Around the Globe*. Toronto, Ontario, Canada: Kids Can Press, 2023.

Solis, Nicholas. *My Town/Mi Pueblo*. New York, NY: Nancy Paulsen Books, 2022.

Websites

Cities
kids.kiddle.co/City
This site includes a fact sheet about cities for kids.

Cities
kids.britannica.com/kids/article/city/352965
Britannica Kids has a Homework Help article about cities for kids with links to vocabulary words.

Rural Areas
kids.kiddle.co/Rural_area
Kiddle provides a fact sheet about rural areas for kids.

Publisher's note to educators and parents: Our editors have carefully reviewed these websites to ensure that they are suitable for students. Many websites change frequently, however, and we cannot guarantee that a site's future contents will continue to meet our high standards of quality and educational value. Be advised that students should be closely supervised whenever they access the internet.

Index

A
agriculture, 15

C
city-states, 22, 23
city council, 16, 17
commute, 10, 11

D
daily lives, 4
downtown, 6, 7, 17

E
environment, 21

F
factories, 7, 24
farms, 13, 14, 15, 22
fire protection, 10, 18

H
homeless shelters, 9

I
Industrial Revolution, 24

M
mayor, 17
Mesopotamia, 22, 23
municipal governments, 16
museums, 7, 18

N
neighbors, 5, 13, 29
New York City, 6, 7, 11, 21

O
online communities, 28

P
police, 10, 17, 18
population, 4, 6, 24, 29

R
religion, 27
rural communities, 4, 5, 9, 12, 13, 14, 15, 19, 20

S
schools, 4, 10, 12, 18, 20, 26
settlers, 22
suburbs, 4, 5, 9, 10, 11, 20, 21, 24, 25

T
taxes, 19
transportation, 20

U
urban communities, 4, 5, 6, 7, 25